THE AR GULF

	miles		
0	100	200	300

	kms	
0	200	400

I R A N

ᴜLF

ingah

Str. of Hormuz

Ras al-Khaimah

Umm al-Qaiwain

Sharjah Ajman

Dubai Fujairah

Abu Dhabi

Al Buraymi

UNITED ARAB

EMIRATES

Muscat

O M A N

Left to right: His Highness Shaikh Zayed bin Sultan Al-Nahayan, Ruler of Abu Dhabi and President of the United Arab Emirates; ESG; His Highness the late Shaikh Rashid bin Saeed Al-Maktoum, Ruler of Dubai, Vice-President and Prime Minister of the United Arab Emirates

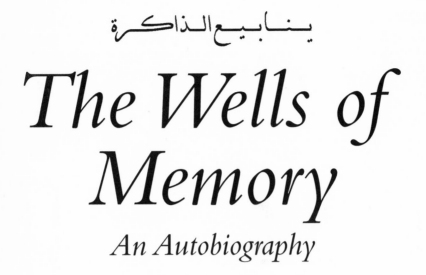

ينـابيـع الـذاكـرة

The Wells of Memory

An Autobiography

Easa Saleh Al-Gurg, CBE

Introduction by
Sir James Craig, GCMG

JOHN MURRAY
Albemarle Street, London

With the editorial collaboration of Michael Rice

© Easa Saleh Al-Gurg 1998

First published in 1998
by John Murray (Publishers) Ltd,
50 Albemarle Street, London W1X 4BD

The moral right of the author has been asserted

A catalogue record for this book is available from the British Library

ISBN 0-7195-5421-7

Typeset in 12/14pt Bembo by Servis Filmsetting Ltd, Manchester
Printed and bound in Great Britain by
The University Press, Cambridge